WHAT DO YOU WANT TO DO BEFORE YOU DIE?

NILESH KUMAR AGARWAL

Copyright © Nilesh Kumar Agarwal
All Rights Reserved.

ISBN 978-1-63974-036-9

This book has been published with all efforts taken to make the material error-free after the consent of the author. However, the author and the publisher do not assume and hereby disclaim any liability to any party for any loss, damage, or disruption caused by errors or omissions, whether such errors or omissions result from negligence, accident, or any other cause.

While every effort has been made to avoid any mistake or omission, this publication is being sold on the condition and understanding that neither the author nor the publishers or printers would be liable in any manner to any person by reason of any mistake or omission in this publication or for any action taken or omitted to be taken or advice rendered or accepted on the basis of this work. For any defect in printing or binding the publishers will be liable only to replace the defective copy by another copy of this work then available.

Contents

Acknowledgements	v
1. Chapter 1	1
Follow Us On Instagram	27

Acknowledgements

First of all, I would like to thank all the people who supported me in completing the book. All these people are unknown to me, but the support that I got, That's really awesome. It is because of you guys that my idea, took a shape of a book. If I remove all of you from the book, then this book will remain just a sheet of paper, nothing else.

When we are young, we have some wishes, when we grow up we still have some wishes. In every moment of life, on every foot, we all have some kind of wish. which varies with time. But there is one wish that we want to fulfill at any cost. To accomplish that we are ready to do anything.

The idea of starting this project was that the wishes of the people should be fulfilled through the power of attraction. Because I do believe in the power of attraction. The more times you read these wishes, the sooner it gets fulfilled.

In this project, you will read such wishes of some special people, which are of utmost importance for them and of course, while reading them you might feel that, oh GOD! this wish is similar to mine. Like the dot mark on the stone never fades away. In the same way, I want people to always remember their wishes so that they get a reminder about them, every time they see this book.

I pray to God that everyone's wish must be fulfilled.

CHAPTER ONE

Sometimes other people dreams make us laugh, tear us up and certainly change our way of thinking. Whether you believe it or not, knowing about other's dreams motivates me for what I want to do in my life. Not every person in this world is capable of creating a goal for himself. But sometimes when we see what another person is doing, we either opt for the same goal or our mind pushes our subconscious mind to think, why we are alive? What is the purpose of our life? It helps you to feel like that, Hey! You are not alone, you are here in this world for something because as per GOD every person is unique in his/her own way. It's about remembering, what actually matters to us when we adopt changes and growth in our life.

Below, I am sharing my favorite responses from the "What do you want to do before you die?" project because these responses have somehow affected my life goals in a positive manner. It really helped me to control my depression. So, I thought I should give it a form of a book so that others could also benefit from it and could see that. Yes, there are other people around too, who also have some kind of goals like you and you just have to find them and build a team to achieve it.

1. Before I die – "I want to help all those women by getting rid of their bully husbands, help them to build their own business and strengthen financially, and not to stay dependent upon those guys who torture them. My nation has plenty of these strong women who are silent and absorbing the pains."

Name: Awesh Gupta
Age: 17
City: Alipurduar (City in West Bengal)

2. Before I die – "To die a martyr. We'll see what happens but I want to be adventurous".

Name: Adnan Shaikh
Age: 19
City: Aurangabad (City in Maharashtra)

3. Before I die – "I wanna make my parents proud n live a successful life.♥?"

Name: Lavanya Dua
Age: 14
City: New Delhi (City in New Delhi)

4. Before I die – " I want to make my parents and country proud"

Name: Shikha Sheth
Age: 22
City: Songadh (City in Gujrat)

5. Before I die – " I just want peace and at least one time in life for a day only want to spend time with me all alone."

Name: Rimpa Chakraborty
Age: 36
City: Jodhpur (City in Rajasthan)

6. Before I die – "I want to perform at a live concert with my most favorite BTS and also want to make as many songs and albums as I can with them.☺"

Name: Nandini Balhara
Age: 17
City: Modinagar (City in Uttar Pradesh)

7. Before I die – "I want to give my mother everything (happiness, respect, fulfillment of her own wishes, freedom, etc.)she deserves, everything that she didn't get even from her parents and her husband (my father) and want to make her feel that she is the happiest person in the whole world, this is the thing I wanna do before I die!"

Name: Maisara Khan
Age: 19
City: Bhopal (City in Madhya Pradesh)

8. Before I die – "I just wanna fulfill my mom dreams"

Name: Shivam Tyagi
Age: 22
City: Meerut (City in Uttar Pradesh)

9. Before I die – "I want to spend the whole day with me only ... eating whatever I like, shopping alone and many other things with only me"

Name: Suhani
Age: 19
City: Meerut (City in Uttar Pradesh)

10. Before I die – "I want to LIVE my life in such a way so that when I'm on my death bed, I won't regret not doing or achieving something, so I made a list of what I want to do, what I want to achieve before I die. As a child growing up in a plain area and watching youtube videos, I always dreamt of trekking on the different mountain ranges and go on different pilgrimages like Vaishno Devi, Gomukh, Gangotri, Tunganath, Amarnath, Kedarnath, Badrinath, Kailash, and Yamunotri.
I want to travel around the world, not for the sake of traveling but to learn- the history, culture, and traditions of these places, to feel the breeze, to lie on the gentle slopes, look at the sky and RELAX. I want to try adventure sports and camping under the open sky. In my pre-teen years, I heard about old-age homes and since then I decided that when I'll start earning and have the freedom to go anywhere, I'll spend time in a nearby old-age home once in a while. Also whatever I want to do, I hope my parents will always be proud of me, as their daughter.
And when I retire, I have decided that I'll leave behind this city life and buy a small house in the countryside and stay there until I die."

Name: Saumili Dutta
Age: 18
City: Kolkata (City in West Bengal)

11. Before I die – "My aim is to spread rich smiles to All the people I know and will further come across and however the other person is to u ....my thing is there is only one life so I'll only treat everyone with love, care and true respect without judging caste, color, creed or

religion.
Like everyone lives for themselves but there should be some who just live to keep others happy."

Name: Adya Dikshit
Age: 20
City: Meerut (City in Uttar Pradesh)

12. Before I die – "So..firstly m apne parents ko proud feel krana chahti hu life m success ho kar then..m apni life m us person ko chahti hu jise pasand krti hu...or filhal wo mere sath nahi hai...but m fir se uske sath hona chahti hu. I dont know why but fir se...."

Name: Shikha Paliwal
Age: 25
City: Meerut (City in Uttar Pradesh)

13. Before I die – "I want to establish a re-habitation center for addicted people"

Name: Tandra Chaki
Age: 34
City: Kaliyaganj (City in West Bengal)

14. Before I die – "I would like to do everything that I'm scared of, bungee jumping diving from a cliff, and more. Also, I would like to leave a mark on this world. I want to tell people that being happy is all that matters"

Name: Sonali Agarwal
Age: 16
City: Gurgaon (City in Haryana)

15. Before I die – "I want to travel every country before I die and I want to own a Rolls Royce Also I want to do farming on a big amount of land."

Name: Aryan Teotia
Age: 17
City: Gandhinagar (City in Gujarat)

16. Before I die – "I want to travel my parents to world tour and also want a world with no borders."

Name: Rajan Kumar
Age: 23
City: Meerut (City in Uttar Pradesh)

17. Before I die – "I want to travel every part of India with my best friend."

Name: Mansi Kansal
Age: 20
City: Meerut (City in Uttar Pradesh)

18. Before I die – "I want to learn surfing and teach it to my dog as well so that I could surf with her."

Name: Shruti Singhal
Age: 23
City: Hapur (City in Uttar Pradesh)

19. Before I die – "I want to do something that will stop rapes for a lifetime."

Name: Sworjjomoy Pathak
Age: 18
City: Bankura (City in West Bengal)

20. Before I die – "I just want to gift my parents all the happiness.. and visit Switzerland with them.. or before gone I want to donate everything that I could ♥?."

Name: Akash Saxena
Age: 21
City: Meerut (City in Uttar Pradesh)

21. Before I die – "I want to be the best fashion designer in the world and let the world praise

me for that. And I collaborate with my favorite ones and I want a part of my earnings to donate to an NGO.
I wanted to fly around the world for the most adventurous sports."

Name: Ipshita Singh
Age: 20
City: Meerut (City in Uttar Pradesh)

22. Before I die – "I want to spend my half salary for NGO, I want to open NGO and spread love and charity with my loved ones."

Name: Akshat Agarwal
Age: 23
City: Meerut (City in Uttar Pradesh)

23. Before I die – "Want to become famous♥? in a good way!"

Name: Sheeba Mary
Age: 29
City: Chennai (City in Tamil Nadu)

24. Before I die – "Want to win muscle building competition, want to become the highest taxpayer of Vapi."

Name: Hiral Jatin Parekh
Age: 38
City: Vapi (City in Gujrat)

25. Before I die – "I think the question is wrong we really don't know when we die so it's better to ask what do we want to do the most when we are alive. For me as long as I'm alive I want to live my life to the fullest and I hope to help others as well. Before I die I want memories of my existence in the minds of my loved ones. When I'm about to die I want to say 'I am happy for my life'."

Name: Ashik Jayan
Age: 19
City: Thrissur (City in Kerala)

26. Before I die – "I want to be an astronaut and want to go to NASA."

Name: Sania
Age: 14
City: Haridwar (City in Uttarakhand)

27. Before I die – "I wish to travel all over the world... And I wished to fulfill my wish as becoming Wildlife Photographer."

Name: SujithaRajalakshmi
Age: 24
City: Theni (Town in Tamil Nadu)

28. Before I die – "I want to travel the world and not I wanna live in the places I am traveling to for some time and I also want to work at United Nations and then retire and live the rest of my life in some remote coastal city of India because there's nothing better than home."

Name: Arpit Chahal
Age: 20
City: Ghaziabad (City in Uttar Pradesh)

29. Before I die – "I want to take care of my parents with the money I earn and fulfill all their wishes and give them love as they gave me."

Name: Taneeshk Ailawadi
Age: 15
City: Ambala (City in Haryana)

30. Before I die – "I want to fulfill my dream to be an author."

Name: Ena Das
Age: 30
City: Chattisgarh (State of India)

31. Before I die – "So maybe that's kind of philosophical but that's what I want :
1 . I want to be a good person and yes that's my goal I don't want to be someone who let their

parents down
2 . I want to be in a good reputed kind of white-collar job
3 . I want to make money so that I can open a dog farm kinda that is in Costa Rica it's too very big but yeah kind of that where I can make strays live
4 . I want to achieve something so that I can leave a legacy I want to be like someone like people know I mean I just not only need money and to be rich even if I don't have money I want people to know me…I hope uh getting my point…I want to get an opportunity once so Ted invites me and I be there giving my speech."

Name: Aayushi Bhasin
Age: 20
City: Haridwar (City in Uttarakhand)

32. Before I die – "A lot of things to do, like a reach at the pinnacle of our career, experience true love, travel as much as u can."

Name: Tanvi Aggarwal
Age: 16
City: Batala (City in Punjab)

33. Before I die – "I just want to fulfill every dream of my parents. As they have seen a lot of struggle in their life. So, just want to give them every happiness they deserve..!!"

Name: Saurabh Verma
Age: 32
City: Meerut (City in Uttar Pradesh)

34. Before I die – "I want to leave in between mountains alone and complete all the Hobbies."

Name: Anushree
Age: 30
City: Rajkot (City in Gujarat)

35. Before I die – "I wanna LIVE before I die… Living is not just eating, sleeping, working, and performing daily activities… I wanna LIVE my life to the fullest? I wanna enjoy each and

every secret of nature, I wanna dance in the Rain, I Wanna Play in Sea, I Wanna Travel the World, I Wanna Learn New Things of Life, I Wanna Be Pure, I Wanna Be a Helping Hand to the needy, I Wanna Cherish each moment of Life... And Most Importantly, I Wanna Do All These Things With My Beloved Life Partner ♥??."

Name: Gayathri Madhan Kumar
Age: 27
City: Hosur (City in Tamil Nadu)

36. Before I die – "I want to do my best and make my parents proud."

Name: Chankita Malhotra
Age: 18
City: Delhi (City in India)

37. Before I die – " 1).Me apni khud ki Identity banana chahti hu ...
2). Kuch log name se mahan hote hai, lekin me name se Nahi Apne kam se mahan banana chahti hu..
3). Apne liye to sabhi log Kuch karte hai lekin me pehle Apne Nahi dushro ke liye Kuch Karna chahti hu ..Jo rasta bhatak Gaye hai unhe help Karna chahti hu..
4)Apne mummy-papa ke sapne pure Karna chahti hu..
5)Itne jyada paise kamana chahti hu ki family ki jaroorat Puri Kar saku or dushro ki help Kar saku..."

Name: Dhokai Archana Mukeshbhai
Age: 23
City: Mithapur, Devbhumi Dwarka (Town in Gujrat)

38. Before I die – "I want to save one life ♥?...I want to give my best contribution to create this beautiful earth one heavenly place existing in this galaxy ....♥? In this age full of inhuman people I want to prove that Yess humanity exists and the truth is the only way to live this life better! Before dying I just want to make myself the best person as ever who will exist in d world ♥?."

Name: Chaitu
Age: 20
City: Nagpur (City in Maharashtra)

39. Before I die – "I'm a crazy girl full of dreams.
I was to be the world's best pop star, go on a world tour.

My concert at different stops in the world.
Perform with my idols my faves and all other artists whose songs meant for me.
Music and fashion are my life and will my life."

Name: Shanaya Singh
Age: 20
City: Delhi (City in India)

40. Before I die – "I want to travel the whole world and open an animal shelter."

Name: Kiran
Age: 28
City: Dehradun (City in Uttarakhand)

41. Before I die – "I want to get answers to questions like 'what is our purpose in our life?", "Where did we come from?" and "Is there life after death?"

Name: Tejas
Age: 14
City: Thane (City in Maharashtra)

42. Before I die – "I need to explore nook n corner of the world."

Name: Miruthula S
Age: 20
City: Coimbatore (City in Tamil Nadu)

43. Before I die – "Fly in a hot air balloon, that experience cannot be described in words, wandering between clouds without any safety harness on your body, feeling the airflow through your body."

Name: Naman Jain
Age: 22
City: Meerut (City in Uttar Pradesh)

44. Before I die – "I want to keep being the person that I am n the names ppl call me(kind-hearted but meek(that's wt they think), grounded but strong-willed, loving but Loving but not real(cause as per them in this day n age u can't genuinely be loving towards everyone)."

Name: Ronica Ambrose Sharma
Age: 33
City: Mohali (City in Punjab)

45. Before I die – "I want to build huge shelter home or farmhouse for orphan dogs, cow, goats, etc. On my own resources without any donation and 2,) wish is to adopt as many as girl child and give them Before my name....."

Name: Leena S Pujara
Age: 35
City: Porbandar (City in Gujarat)

46. Before I die – "So the things I want to do before I die are as follows:
• wanna travel all seven continents.
• wanna have a thrilling adventure by climbing mt. Everest.
• wanna publish my first book which will be my own biopic in the form of poems and verses
• wanna realize my dreams
• wanna fall in love n then get cheated by my boyfriend just to gain experience
• wanna play my guitar all over the world
• wanna get a small house between woods just to experience horrific events in real
• wanna have the wildest bath with my loved one.
• wanna get into tribal communities during my journey in the Amazon rainforest and escape from there without getting harm
• last but not the least wanna have a silent death without any pain.............."

Name: Palak
Age: 19
City: Meerut (City in Uttar Pradesh)

47. Before I die – "World tour."

Name: Suhani
Age: 18
City: Kota (City in Rajasthan)

48. Before I die – "I want to ride bike freely with my girl gang without any fear from men at night, also I want to ride in a hot air balloon at least once."

Name: Prerna Sai Shaw
Age: 23
City: Meerut (City in Uttar Pradesh)

49. Before I die – "I want to fulfill all my dreams and make my parents proud and contribute to India's development. That is my wish and my only aim for which I came to this world."

Name: Simran
Age: 19
City: Bhubaneshwar (City in Odisha)

50. Before I die – "मै लापरवाह होना चहाती बिल्कुल बेपरवाह आसमान की एक छोटी बदली की तरह कि हवाए जहां चाहें ले जायें बस मैं मस्ती में बहती चलूं बेखोफ सी........"

Name: Garima
Age: 29
City: Meerut (City in Uttar Pradesh)

51. Before I die – "There is a list of things I wanted to do but I will tell you some specific things which I absolutely wanted to do first of all I wanna make my parents proud of me by becoming a CA, I wanted to go on a mountain and scream as loud as I can, wanted to marry the guy I love and have a little cute daughter♥?."

Name: Rashi
Age: 20
City: Meerut (City in Uttar Pradesh)

52. Before I die – "I want to be successful and create a safe workplace for women so it becomes easy for them to follow their dreams despite their gender."

Name: Summaiya Ansari
Age: 27
City: Meerut (City in Uttar Pradesh)

53. Before I die – "India I want to travel the world - walk on the iconic streets, trek, do adventure sports, explore new destinations, revisit a few of them with a new perspective again, learn different cultures and above all, unpause and reclaim the lost time."

Name: Dr. Trisheetaa Tej
Age: 34
City: Hyderabad (City in Telangana)

54. Before I die – "I want to live a life, which is more interesting than a Hollywood super hit movie!
I want to make a difference(positive) in the lives of the people so that their life can change for the betterment!
I want to do something or everything, by which my ideals, my mentors become my FANS!
I want to create a nation where people can grow as an individual and can love their country, their religion, their people and of course themselves, which is the requirement of an hour in my country!
Before I die I want to become the supporting shoulder to a lady, who wants to pursue her dreams and who wants to be addressed by her name, not just by somebody else's mother or wife or daughter!
I can go on writing and writing about what I need to do before I die!"

Name: Rupali Chaudhary
Age: 20
City: Aligarh (City in Uttar Pradesh)

55. Before I die – "Want to fulfill my wishlist,
N I started working on it... rather die in regret ...I want to do acting."

Name: Rachana Vasavada
Age: 36
City: Mumbai (City in Maharashtra)

56. Before I die – "I wanna get my caricature made plus try bungee jumping ....and experience the night life of Paris....just once ...alone."

Name: Nandini
Age: 18
City: Meerut (City in Uttar Pradesh)

57. Before I die – "I want to do more help to people's who want.... And I service to orphanage people."

Name: Keerthana
Age: 26
City: NA (City in Tamilnadu)

58. Before I die – "I want to do something which can make my family and loved ones feel proud . Like teaching kids who lives in slum area ,when they will be educated by me and later they can remember my name and say proudly I am student of Apar Gupta."

Name: Apar Gupta
Age: 22
City: Meerut (City in Uttar Pradesh)

59. Before I die – "I have a dream to open a public library on my own on a large scale with cafe."

Name: Mansi Garg
Age: 47
City: Meerut (City in Uttar Pradesh)

60. Before I die – "World tour All seven continents."

Name: Isha Sharma
Age: 37
City: Jaipur (City in Rajasthan)

61. Before I die – "Wanna be a singer And a writer."

Name: Deepak Rana
Age: 23
City: Meerut (City in Uttar Pradesh)

62. Before I die – "Well I mostly want to go to America
But my favorite city there is LA (Los Angeles)
The reason I like this city so much is because well it has beaches I love and it's a city where my dreams may come true (can't tell u the dreams but I guess this will do)
And I like New York too cause it's kinda fascinating."

Name: Masumi
Age: 18
City: Meerut (City in Uttar Pradesh)

63. Before I die – "I want to become an IAS officer and want to travel India."

Name: Saurabh Singh
Age: 22
City: Meerut (City in Uttar Pradesh)

64. Before I die – "I want to change this society for the sake of girls, I have so many goals
But changing this society is the first one."

Name: K. B. Priya
Age: 18
City: Changes city once in 2 years (India)

65. Before I die – "Want to become a rich businessman and tour of the whole world with family on a business visa."

Name: Khizar
Age: 16
City: Meerut (City in Uttar Pradesh)

66. Before I die – "I want to know what happens when we die before I die."

Name: Shahrukh Shaikh
Age: 22
City: Sikar (City in Rajasthan)

67. Before I die – "I want to visit all beautiful north cities of my country India, roam, explore places, monuments, rich history, people and food. It's my only wish."

Name: Nivedita
Age: 25
City: NA (INDIA)

68. Before I die – "Live a beautiful life that I can remember after I die."

Name: Srinithaa
Age: 14
City: Chennai (City in Tamil Nadu)

69. Before I die – "Duniya ghumna chahti hun. Before die I want to make my career successful so that I can do anything that I want to do in my life. No rules no regulations. I fond of traveling. I just love traveling to different places, Mainly mountains. Right now my destination places are Kedarnath, Manali, Kasol, Shimla, Kashmir, Darjeeling, Ladakh many more places. I love to explore myself I want to know about my country what is the good thing about the place and why? If I got a chance to go out of the country then I would like to go to Switzerland..."

Name: Monika Chaudhary
Age: 23
City: Meerut (City in Uttar Pradesh)

70. Before I die – "1. I want to serve the country by joining the most prestigious organization The Indian Army.
2. I want to explore and experience this beautiful world with my close friends and family.
3. I want to contribute to the field of education and in making this world a better place.
4. Embrace and enjoy every moment of my life."

Name: Prinsa Kathait
Age: 23
City: Dehradun (City in Uttarakhand)

71. Before I die – "I want to climb Mt. Everest with my loved one...."

Name: Archana Subramaniam
Age: 25
City: Coimbatore (City in Tamil Nadu)

72. Before I die – "I just want to help needy people's lives..cause der are tonnes of people without daily needs."

Name: M.sandhiya Devi
Age: 24
City: Coimbatore (City in Tamil Nadu)

73. Before I die – "I want to be a perfect entrepreneur as a lady wid smart thinking."

Name: Megha Khanna
Age: 36
City: Bareilly (City in Uttar Pradesh)

74. Before I die – "Make a difference even if it's a small one."

Name: Megha Kansal
Age: 22
City: Ahemdabad (City in Gujrat)

75. Before I die – "Want to be happy, just Happy...."

Name: Divya Chavda
Age: 21
City: Surat (City in Gujrat)

76. Before I die – "I want to witness the northern lights with my parents and want them to remember that moment for a lifetime. And I want to picture that moment."

Name: Shivendra Kumar Kungarwal
Age: 22
City: Meerut (City in Uttar Pradesh)

77. Before I die – "I just want to become a person that I love and that would be like someone who would learn about the earth. its inhabitants, its nature, greenery, oceans, humans, animals, and life. Who would travel into space ? and explore what's beyond the reach of the homo sapiens."

Name: Shubhi Tomar
Age: 18
City: Meerut (City in Uttar Pradesh)

78. Before I die – "I really wanna tell all my feelings and emotions which I never told to my dad and mom ♥?."

Name: Krushika Reddy Bhavanam
Age: 21
City: Warangal (City in Telangana)

79. Before I die – " I want to fix the problems between my parents before I die."

Name: Umme habiba
Age: 22
City: Bilepasar (City in Karnataka)

80. Before I die – "I just want to convey a message to all the people of India then I can die peacefully at any time."

Name: Kartavya
Age: NA
City: NA (City in INDIA)

81. Before I die – "I wanna go Korea and meet BTS."

Name: Shivani
Age: NA
City: NA (City in INDIA)

82. Before I die – "I want to be a cricketer and want to open a cricket academy for children who can't afford their own cricket kit but want to be a cricketer."

Name: Ujjwal Poonia
Age: 12
City: NA (City in INDIA)

83. Before I die – " I would want to make sure there is no misunderstanding between people closer to me so that when I turn to dust, they don't regret."

Name: Arya Kadhattarwal
Age: NA
City: NA (City in INDIA)

84. Before I die – "Before I die I want to serve my parents as much as I can and make there dreams come true. Mai chahti hu ki is duniya me koi doctor na ho, kisi ko bhi doctor hone ki zaroorat na pare. Aur ye doctor ki koi job ya padhayi hi na ho. I want to make a medicine which can heal every wound and injury a birth vaccine, Jo baby ko lagane he bad zindagi bhar use koi bimari na ho, aur is duniya me sabhi healthy rahe kisi ko doctor ki zaroorat na pare ."

Name: Fatima Sultan
Age: 15
City: NA (City in INDIA)

85. Before I die – "I want to be acknowledged for raising my children as better citizens of the society."

Name: Deepa Darsana
Age: NA
City: NA (City in INDIA)

86. Before I die – "I want to give My mom & dad happiness & rest and I am complete his or her every wish .whatever they want everything. I want to go to Vrindavan and in front of Kanha Ji take my last breath."

Name: Vidushi Sain
Age: 26
City: Meerut (City in Uttar Pradesh)

87. Before I die – "Before I die I want to donate all my organs and do a thing by which my name can be updated in the book of world record."

Name: Bandana Choubey
Age: 14
City: Siliguri (City in West Bengal)

88. Before I die – "Live for myself ♥?."

Name: Tejaswini
Age: NA
City: NA (City in INDIA)

89. Before I die – "I just wanna fulfill my wishes."

Name: Devyanshi
Age: NA
City: NA (City in INDIA)

90. Before I die – "I want to visit the whole world with joy n enthusiasm, there are no worries in the surroundings when we (family) are on a world tour... ."

Name: Priyanka Bhawsar
Age: 26
City: Ujjain (City in Madhya Pradesh)

91. Before I die – "I want to become that much successful person that I make a shelter for the poor and needy, who resides along the footpath in every district I used to live."

Name: Sapna Verma
Age: 25
City: Meerut (City in Uttar Pradesh)

92. Before I die – "To achieve my dreams."

Name: Manisha
Age: 21
City: NA (City in INDIA)

93. Before I die – "Lot of things."

Name: Nancy Kaushik
Age: NA
City: NA (City in INDIA)

94. Before I die – "I would like to live the life to the fullest.
Today, we as a social being are so bound by our social duty that we actually tend to forget what we as an individual desire or wish.
Being a child, we actually don't know what we actually desire...we bend towards the fancy thing or is actually more driven by the mates we have
When we grow up....we are busier in making our career.
And becomes old enough that we become a social being that we have to fulfill our social duty and the life goes on and on
Sometimes people recognize that they have to live life and not just go with the flow.
So here, by living to the fullest means that I don't want to repent on the last day that I have not done that...I want to do all I desire to do Live life to the fullest."

Name: Sommya Jindal
Age: 22
City: NA (City in INDIA)

95. Before I die – "World tour."

Name: Vaibhav
Age: 25
City: Meerut (City in Uttar Pradesh)

96. Before I die – "I want to explore the world before I die ?? Travelling the unseen and getting to know different cultures."

Name: Satya Giri
Age: 23
City: NA (City in INDIA)

100. Before I die – "I want to travel to space and do sex in zero gravity."

Name: Harsh
Age: 19
City: NA (City in INDIA)

101. Before I die – "To adopt minimum 100 children's and provide them education, better life and acknowledge them with the concept of the world is one."

Name: Dushyant Saxena
Age: 27
City: NA (City in INDIA)

102. Before I die – "I want to be a healer and meet Ashwatthama once."

Name: Shilpa Agarwal
Age: 45
City: NA (City in INDIA)

103. Before I die – "I want to be a researcher and also explore different places and cultures. Want to spread smile to those who think that they cant smile again."

Name: Keerthana Raghunath
Age: 25
City: NA (City in INDIA)

104. Before I die – "I would like to play at least a small part of my role to society. My lifetime goal is to plant more saplings and to see my happiness of mine in others' smiles. I'm waiting for my time to spread love and happiness like the fragrance of flowers everywhere on this holy earth. Still, I know that there is a huge milestone in my path to reach the destination, until then I wait for the right time with patience by adding colorfulness and allowing it to fly in the sky of my dreams. Hard work with smart work allows reaching the destination. I take this as my mantra to reach the dream of mine."

Name: P.Elavarasi
Age: 25
City: NA (City in INDIA)

105. Before I die – "I want to become a playback singer."

Name: Spandana
Age: 29
City: NA (City in INDIA)

106. Before I die – "The answer to your question is a long travel without no destination with the person whom my heart and soul loves.no and regulations. Thank you for your question I was thinking of more answers."

Name: Ignatius
Age: NA
City: NA (City in INDIA)

107. Before I die – "To make my parents feel the luckiest parent. It's so simple it's not that complicated like doing for me or doing for them......it's just the respect you have in society. As you know at present we are known by our parent's name...like he or she is their son daughter.....but the day when someone introduces your parents by your name like....they are Nilesh Authors parent.......I promise this line will touch their heart...that they are now recognized by their child's name...."

Name: Jatin Abusaria
Age: 19
City: NA (City in INDIA)

108. Before I die – "I want to make a fully organic farmhouse which produces no (non-biodegradable)waste. Where energy is harness from wind and solar energy and later that model can be applied to cities."

Name: Arvind K. Patir
Age: 23
City: Sikar (City in Rajasthan)

109. Before I die – "I want to live at least once before I die rather than existing."

Name: Veronica
Age: NA
City: NA (City in INDIA)

110. Before I die – "I want to open a private ZOO & marry to SHAMPOO (dog)."

Name: Mahima Fageria
Age: 22
City: NA (City in Rajasthan)

111. Before I die – "To be happy 24hrs....without any single worries even for a single second."

Name: OVIYA
Age: 18
City: NA (City in INDIA)

112. Before I die – "I want to find love and peace and true joy and happiness And I want to help the animals, and give them joy and freedom, as much as I can And above all true love it is, I m so tired of feeling this torment."

Name: NA
Age: 22
City: NA (City in INDIA)

113. Before I die – "I want to be an air hostess and travel the whole world being an air hostess."

Name: Swatilekha Dey
Age: 27
City: NA (City in INDIA)

114. Before I die – "Want to settle my family as a freedom of financial."

Name: Sangeetha Sanjana
Age: 22
City: Tindivanam (Town in Tamil Nadu)

115. Before I die – "I want to fulfill all the dreams of my Dad and Mom."

Name: Nehal Shamim
Age: 30
City: Kolkata (City in West Bengal)

116. Before I die – "A DREAM. A WISH. THESE WORDS OFTEN SEND ME INTO A WHIRLWIND OF EMOTIONS. BEING AN ARIES, THE THOUGHT OF DEATH SEEMS LIKE A HEARTBREAK. WHAT'S EVEN WORSE IS THE THOUGHT OF OBLIVION. IT'S JUST THAT ONE DAY ALL OF THIS WILL BE A WASTELAND. THIS GORGEOUS EMPIRE THAT I'VE WORKED TO BUILD ALL MY LIFE, WILL CEASE TO EXIST IN JUST A SECOND. THE VERY MOMENT THE WIND STEALS MY BREATH, IT WILL CRUMBLE INTO DUST AND SILENCE WILL SURROUND THE VERY LAND THAT MEANT EVERYTHING TO ME. THESE THOUGHTS REMIND ME TO LIVE WHILE I CAN. EVERY TIME SOMEONE ASKS ME WHAT I WANT TO DO BEFORE I DIE, I'M NOT ABLE TO DECIDE WHAT TO ANSWER. BUT IF I HAVE TO BE HONEST, I WANT TO FEEL EVERY SENSATION, I WANT TO HEAR EVERY SONG, I WANT TO TRAVEL TO EACH NOOK AND CORNER OF THIS WORLD. AND THOUGH IT IS IMPOSSIBLE, I WANT TO EXPERIENCE BEING EVERYTHING. FROM A DOCTOR TO AN ARTIST. FROM A MILLIONAIRE TO A HOMELESS. I WANT TO LOOK THROUGH EACH AND EVERY ONE POINT OF VIEW. I WANT TO TRY EVERY SINGLE DISH EVER COOKED; I WANT TO BE A PART OF EVERY CULTURE TO EXIST. I WANT TO LEARN EVERY SINGLE INSTRUMENT AND READ EVERY SINGLE BOOK. I WANT TO WATCH EVERY SINGLE SERIES AND I WANT TO ENJOY EVERY SINGLE MOVIE. I WANT TO MEET EVERY SINGLE PERSON IN THIS WORLD. I WANT TO LIVE LIFE AS A QUEEN, THEN AS A PEASANT. I WANT TO LIVE IN EACH ERA. I WANT TO SEE THE WORLD GROW AND GROW WITH IT. I WANT TO BE THE ARCHER AND I ALSO WANT TO BE THE PREY. I WANT TO LEAVE AND I WANT TO STAY. THERE IS NO SINGLE THING I WANT TO DO BEFORE I DIE. I WANT TO BE FREE, LIKE A PHOENIX. I WANT TO FLY AND COME BACK STRONGER EACH TIME I FALL. I WANT TO BE FIERCE AND

PASSIONATE. I WANT TO BE BOLD AND BEAUTIFUL. I WANT TO STAY OUT OF THE CHAINS, THOUGH BRUISED AND RAGGED, I WANT TO FIGHT. THOUGH FORBIDDEN, I WANT TO LOVE. I WANT TO DRINK WITH THE STARS AND VOYAGE THROUGH GALAXIES. I WANT TO BE EVERY CHARACTER FROM EVERY BOOK. THOUGH TRAGIC, I WANT TO LIVE AND FACE EVERYTHING THAT COMES MY WAY. I KNOW ONE DAY ILL HAVE TO LEAVE ALL THIS COLOUR AND BEAUTY BEHIND BUT YET I WANT TO BUILD THE MOST BEAUTIFUL MANSION IF ONLY TO SEE IT CRUMBLE BEFORE MY OWN EYES. THE IRONY OF LIFE IS THAT IT UNPREDICTABLE AND I PLAN TO CHALLENGE IT INTO A DUEL AND RISK LOSING EVERYTHING OR PERHAPS HAVE ALL THAT I WANT."

Name: Charvi Dhiran
Age: 15
City: Chennai (City in Tamil Nadu)

117. Before I die – "I want to become a woman of values and knowledge which I can share as much as possible....also I want to help people in my own way....and be a successful entrepreneur."

Name: Swarnima Shrivastava
Age: 40
City: Indore (City in Madhya Pradesh)

118. Before I die – "I would like to go to Australia."

Name: Sangeetha
Age: 30
City: NA (City in Tamil Nadu)

119. Before I die – "I want that my parents feel proud of me before I die And I also want an understanding soulmate."

Name: Saloni
Age: 18
City: Meerut (City in Uttar Pradesh)

Follow Us On Instagram

An initiative by STAALLION FOUNDATION MEERUT

We plan and prepare for most events of our lifetime, yet few of us prepare for that final event.

The ultimate gift of peace we can give to us is to make our wishes known in writing.

Thank you for doing this for yourself.

www.ingramcontent.com/pod-product-compliance
Lightning Source LLC
LaVergne TN
LVHW081530060526
838200LV00049B/2274